FOR THE REST OF TIME

ULRICH KELLERER

FOR THE REST OF TIME

How to Live Your Best Life

Bibliographical information from the German National Library
The German National Library has registered this publication
in the German National Bibliography. You can find detailled
bibliographical information by visiting http://dnb.dnb.de.

Table of contents

Moments are the only thing we have
We don't remember the years or months of our lives. We
only remember moments.

The art of living resides in the ability to enjoy the moment.
It is all we ever have. Life is a journey to yourself. The choice
to take that journey leads to an exciting life. The greatest
challenge is to be able to deal with yourself.

Every morning you get up with yourself and at night you go
to bed with yourself too. In between those two moments we
meet other people such as family, friends and work colleagues.
If you can't stand yourself, you will have a hard time standing
others too.

That is why it is important how you start your day. Your
attitude toward life is crucial. If you have a positive attitude,
you are on the right path toward a fulfilling life.

Make the right decisions and be the capitan of your own ship
called "life." If others are in charge of your life instead, you
will lead a second-hand life. Move beyond your comfort zone
and enter the miracle called "life."

We only have one life so don't push things off until tomorrow. Tomorrow is uncertain and yesterday is long gone. You
only have the here and now. When people talk about what
they will do "some day," they are pushing their lives off for
another day.

We have a plan for everything. The most important one, however, is your life.

Create your master plan!

Where am I from and where do I want to go?

What are my greatest dreams in life?

How can I make them come true?

Who can help me on my path?

What is my big "why" in life?

Am I living my life's purpose or am I still searching for it?

Does my family support me?

Do I have friends who will support me to reach my goals?

Do I have a job or a calling?

Self-discovery

It all starts with consciousness and becoming aware of what is really important in your life. Then you have to take action to realize your plans and goals.

Are you the creator of your life and have you taken it upon yourself to shape your life according to your wishes?

Start to fill your life with great experiences and moments and look forward to every single day. Be creative and have fun on your life's journey. If you are doing well, then you also contribute to others because we should live our destiny and act with compassion as human beings. A successful collaboration allows us to experience the meaning of life and gives us the strength to enjoy and experience the gift of life to the fullest.

In order to be motivated in your own life, it is helpful to hearstories of other people who have mastered the moments of life positively, thereby providing a good example.

May the following stories inspire you and help you experience life's most precious moments:

One story that I experienced as a child has stuck with me all these years. My father was a local editor in our city in the south of Munich. His work was his life. For him, the newspaper was everything he always wanted. But he worked long hours and smoked 60 cigarettes a day. He became more and more hoarse until we could hardly understand him anymore. He categorically refused to go to the doctor until it was nearly too late.

When he finally went to the doctor, the diagnosis was devastating: throat cancer!

He had come much too late, the doctors said, and an emergency operation was essential. The operation was performed shortly afterwards in Munich.

Coincidentally, our school class had planned a trip to the opera in Munich at the same time, providing me with a perfect opportunity for me to leave the classroom inconspicuously and make my way to the clinic to see my father.

When I saw him in his bed, newly operated, I was completely shocked. He had a hole in his throat and was trying to speak somehow. He couldn't make a single sound and could only blow air through the hole in his throat.

My father also panicked when he realized that I did not understand him. Robbed of his voice, which was the most important thing in his life, it was like a horror movie unfolding. As hard as I tried, I couldn't understand what my father wanted to tell me.

Shocked and exhausted, I ran down the hospital corridor back to my classmates.

My father, however, was a strong fighter and so he managed to speak and even talk on the phone again with a device.

But the illness was too far advanced and he died without hope after a long period of suffering.

So I was already without a father at the age of 18 and could never ask him for his advice again, with all the decisions that were pending in my young life.

As a result of losing my father early, I developed the ability to listen to my inner voice and to sharpen my intuition.

Somehow I always felt guided by more than just a feeling of confidence and determination. Since I myself was hospitalized seven times in two years with the diagnosis "acute pancreatitis," a disease that had put me in a coma two years prior, I had a near-death experience there, which was the most beautiful thing I ever had.

There were colors and a music that does not exist here on earth and I came to a gate and a voice asked me if I wanted to go through the gate or back to life.

Immediately I knew that it must be God and it was so wonderful that I wanted to go through the gate immediately. But I was sixteen years old and wanted to tell this story to my parents and my girlfriend.

Miraculously, I woke up after four days in a coma and was back to life. Ever since I had this great experience, I have no longer been afraid that I might die, only of the way I might die itself. There is so much more around us and within us that no one has to be afraid.

Of course, I could not finish school with the necessary degree due to my many hospital stays and life took another direction.

I am convinced that if you have enough faith and trust, life will always lead you in the right direction. Be brave. Get involved in the great miracle LIFE and enjoy the journey to yourself.

Take it with humor!

Life is too short and only if you live consciously and intensely will you be able to enjoy the treasures of life and the precious moments. It is never too late to start something new and if you listen to the voice in your heart, you will have as many happy moments as you wish.

Listen to your inner voice rather than the opinions of others!

You may live your life according to your own ideas and should not always want to please others.

Find the right life partner and go through the adventure of LIFE together with him.

Motivate and inspire each other and realize that love is the greatest force on earth.

Give love and affection and you will also be loved.

Life writes the best stories. Get involved.

Have fun!

Life's purpose

Find out what your life's purpose is. Be brave and trust your inner voice. It accompanies you your whole life and always knows exactly what is right for you. A faithful companion on the way to your wishes and dreams!

Open your heart wide and inhale this new awareness of life. Let your life become an adventure and don't let others distract you from your path.

You can achieve and create everything if you believe in yourself and are ready to go the extra mile to happiness.

So many people have achieved their goals and you can do anything. Every journey begins with the first step and on your way, you will experience exciting things. Experiences and memories are all we take with us.

From the very first moment of life, you begin to write your own life story.

How does your day begin?

What habits and rituals do you have? How consciously do you start each new day?

To hold the steering wheel of life in your hands in an externally controlled world has almost become an exception. We are all driven by life and try to become faster and faster in our activities.

No stopping, no reflecting. Rushing and continuing, whatever the cost!

The outside world has us firmly in its grip, although we know that all happiness comes from within. Who wants to confront themselves with that truth?

So forge ahead, close your eyes and keep going until at some point somewhere something happens that forces us to change the course we have taken.

"One moment can change your life!"

Then suddenly everything is different. Then we feel powerless and helpless. Then it takes humility and trust that everything will end well. Why does something always have to happen first so that we wake up and realize how vulnerable we are?

Of course, we have long since built up a facade for the outside world and of course we can react to the "circus of life" depending on the situation.

But how do we feel about it?

How far have we moved away from ourselves? How much life do we feel inside ourselves?

To set out to play in the arena of life, take the box seats and be a part of the big event! We want to, but so many things hold us back, including our constant excuses. The explanations about why something won't work or is not possible. Have we really tried and if so, how often? Don't we always give up too early and have the answer at hand why it won't work?

As a result, we become more and more passive and enjoy the life of others on TV, magazines and YouTube. We take refuge in social media and post nice glossy positive pictures. A life from the backseat.

Just like at school! Don't stand out and go along with the crowd. It's like the ships that are halfway to the harbor. But that's not what they're built for.

Cast off the lines and sail into your adventure called LIFE. It will captivate you and lead you to new insights.

There is so much more out there. At best we are sailing at twenty percent of our capacity. It's like a technical device. Most of what is in the manual we don't even use.

Fears and doubts always hold us back and our minds hold us captive with negative thoughts. Ninety percent of our fears never come true.

What's the worst case scenario? Not having tried it!

That is the core message of this book.

Try something and it's never too late to start over.

What are you waiting for?

For the right moment? It never comes!

Start now and go ahead. It's not the speed that counts; it's that you lead the way. You can change direction, but you have to take action.

Don't observe how others live, but shape your life anew every day.

Set a good example. We are all influenced by others and yet we know so little about each other. Our perception is what makes the difference here.

We see things the way we would like to see them. In truth, we create our own reality. Positive affirmations and visualizations help us to do this.

Creator of life

Imagine what you would like and give your thoughts power and feeling. This way they have the tendency to become reality. Your thoughts form your reality.

You are what you think.

Be the creator of your life. There are few who are interested in you shaping your life tomorrow and claiming to think and act for yourself.

It is more acceptable when we all simply hold our nose to the grindstone. Then we are predictable and manipulable. What we think, eat, calculate, believe and for whom we vote. Please be predictable so that everything is under control! Just don't cut yourself off from the manipulated masses. Just don't go your own way.

Change upsets others because they want to be able to assess you as they know you and as predictable as you are.

But life is all about change!

Nothing remains as it is. Only through change is evolution possible. If everything remained as it was, it would mean you are at a standstill, which leads to death.

"Be the change you want to see in the world," Gandhi said.

 Yes, to want to make this contribution and to get involved and take responsibility, to look toward the future and not look away.

Don't think: "Well, it'll be too much for me."

To think it would be nice if the kids got something from planet Earth and we didn't selfishly destroy everything first. If we are not careful today with the available resources, we will not have a future.

The sun is shining for everyone, but our life is on a lease; it is only on loan to us.

On the day of our reckoning, we have to take stock of what the price of life has been.

Life is a gift and gifts are not defined by price, but by value. Live a life full of value, be mindful and have respect for life and its creatures.

Everything is possible and you often cannot imagine the best in your wildest dreams. Believe in something and believe in yourself, then the universe will give you the necessary tools to master your life.

What if you only had half a year left to live? What would change that and what would be important and right for you then?

Don't wait for tomorrow!

Start today. Start NOW!

Even the smallest things can have a great impact. Everyone can start with a baby step.

Make a plan as you would with a "to-do list." Write down what you want to change, what your goals and desires are.

By when do you want to achieve this and that and, above all, why?

Who can optimally support you on your path and above all, do you have the courage to ask for help?

So many people are happy to help, if only they are asked. We all like to pass on life experience, but you have to ask.

Only then will the others open up and help you achieve your goals and dreams. We are nothing alone. We need the support of others. We are not alone with our problems, fears and doubts.

We all swirl on the path of life and we all have our ups and downs. Overcoming them and taking the right course is the task before you.

Never give up and continue!

How often did you have the feeling that now I have to change something?

Change my life toward a new course? Do something different?

Second thoughts

What keeps holding us back?

So-called second thoughts, worries and fears that something might not work out as we think and that we will make a fool of ourselves because we will fail anyway.

Does that sound like a self-determined life?

Are we here to be afraid or is it finally time to say "yes" to ourselves and to life?

How distant have you become from yourself and life? Isn't it time to make a change of course?

If you succeed, a new life lies ahead of you. You will not regret anything and you will know that everything is all right now.

Being in the right place at the right time is the art of living in the here and now. No waiting for tomorrow.

Start now with something you have always wanted to do yet have forgotten how important it is for you.

"Go for it!"

Your passion will return and lead you forward without budget and business plan, but to be part of it with joy and to work again on something that corresponds to your own nature in an ultimate state of flow. To do something with and out of love is the big difference to the drive of our everyday life.

To bring a splash of color into your life again and to make the images in your mind come to life on the canvas.

Don't wait for answers from the media, but hear the inner voice, listen and instinctively do the right thing, just like in nature. Life has a plan. He who sows apples cannot harvest pears.

What do you want to sow? Self-determination? Satisfaction? Happiness? Health?

Your calling

Turn your hobby into your profession and your profession into your vocation. Sail away from the safe harbor and discover the world. Time is finite in this world, but you can become the hero of your own story.

The hero of your life – courageous and strong – with new goals every day. Life is a journey that leads to more than just yourself.

Create a master plan for the day, week, month, year and, ultimately, your entire life.

What is there left to do and experience?

What is your list of unrealized dreams?

What do you have to change to get closer to your heart's desire?

The habits you have are deeply entrenched and automatically repeat themselves every day. You can replace an old habit with a new one in just three weeks when you practice new behaviors.

Don't be afraid of change! Have courage to try out new things. Everything is right before you. It is up to you to set out to experience all the miracles and happy moments life has to offer. How often do we say we don't have enough time or money to try new things?

Job commitments and family obligations often hinder us from trying out new things. The truth is we packed our life's baggage ourselves.

We can eliminate certain things in order to provide room for new things. Get up an hour earlier or go to bed an hour earlier.

Change your routine for new things and experiences.

How did you learn in school? Through repetition!

How do you learn new habits? Through repetition!

If you try something new and are successful in doing so, repeat! Every new beginning brings its own set of challenges, but when it becomes automatic, things seem to run on their own.

When you have found your rhythm, it's all about "doing it." You no longer have to spend your energy thinking about it. It happens involuntarily.

At some point, this is no longer a challenge. We want and need something new. To do so, we have to create space and time to integrate it into our routine.

It has to come from the inside to manifest itself on the outside. Waiting is not an option.

The world continues to turn without us. No one is waiting. Jump in and share in your life adventure story.

Do it!

Doing one thing every day will accomplish more than you can imagine in five years. The engine of life is waiting for you to turn it on and begin the journey. Forward is what drives us and forward is the only direction you can take in your life.

Backwards is only in thoughts and memories. No matter how fast you go, the main thing is to move forward.

Everything flows; everything has a reason and a cause. You don't have to be spiritual, but it would help you to understand things and causes better. Familiar and supposedly safe paths are well known, but the adventure begins on paths we have never walked before. The closed doors can only be opened when we are ready to conquer new territory.

Behind the hill lies the promised land, in front of it the difficult path. Every step brings you closer to your goal and your courage will be rewarded at the end of the journey and not at its beginning.

Think of the courage of the early sailors and discoverers and how little they knew what to expect. When the vision is big enough, the courage to take this path comes. Today's GPS shows us where we are in the world and how long it will take to reach your destination.

Our inner voice tells us that if we trust in it, we will reach our goal, but this is much more exciting because it is not always predictable.

Why consume the adventure only on TV or in the cinema? Why not make a film of your own life and experience it?

It is only one life and as I said, it is over too quickly. Therefore, consciously recognize what it's all about and as I said, it's never too late for something new.

Lead the dialogue with yourself and listen to yourself. You will always get the right answers to the questions of your heart.
"Nothing happens without a reason!"

When you realize what you can influence with your concerns and actions, you will never again just live into the day.

Passion and willpower will drive you forward to never imagined possibilities. Everything works if you believe in it and work on it. Life loves heroes. Be one of them!

Who puts the most pressure on you?

You yourself in an effort to fulfill your expectations!

Expectations from whom? Your boss? Family? Friends?

Letting go, meditation, sports, yoga, power walking...

There are so many ways to provide you with useful things to help you live a powerful, self-determined life. A time-out, sabbatical, silent monastery or the Way of St. James.

So much is waiting for you to feel your inner self again and to enjoy the joy of life.

Our dependencies and addictions such as alcohol etc. stand in the way of achieving our goals. We remain predictable and give up the big dreams for the small desires. The inner voice, however, comes back and it is up to you to listen to it or ignore it.

There are many things we cannot influence e.g. the weather. But we can always influence how we react to it.

Karma is not what happens to you, but how you react to it. One door closes and another one opens.

The question is where do you want to go and why? What drives you?

What else is missing on your list of life?

Let's see?

I don't know.

Depends? etc.

No vague, wishy washy answers allowed!

Commitment

Americans call it "commitment."

Consider it a pact you make with yourself.

Say "yes" to your dreams and plans and really consider what you want.

It is not about being selfish toward others. Instead, it is about self-determination and being the captain of your own life – the so-called *Capitano della Vita*. Switch on the GPS toward a new life and new happiness.

How wonderful it feels and how wonderful to finally try it? Where have you been so long?

What stopped you and what kept you away?

Anyway, now you are wide awake and brave. So now it really starts. Step by step toward a new direction. Bravo!

They say you grow with the tasks you are given. I believe your courage gives you strength and confidence, maybe even wings. As long as there is still music inside you, play your song over and over again.

This is your new life; this is your new freedom. Soon it will be as natural as it should be. Oh, and another thing: Do you love secrets?

Then make your new life a secret. You don't have to tell everyone what you are up to and which dreams you want to realize now.

Keep this secret to yourself. It is your adventure and your way. If you tell others about it, they will talk you out of it and find 1000 reasons why it will not work. Others want to have you as they know and can judge you. Please do not change your mind now.

So rather than ridicule yourself and have a midlife crisis. Stay with us, it's all good, which you can translate as being manageable and predictable.

First of all, it's not what you think. Nothing will happen to you.

Nature, life and the universe function according to rules and laws. It's like the wind. You can have it for or against you.

There is no magic word, but a chance for everyone who tries something new. Be a pioneer and explorer.

Have you ever done a fasting cure? Therapeutic Lent? Over several days, nothing but water and tea. Maybe a soup!

Has your body not shown what it is capable of and what it needs or does not need? You must have felt better afterwards.

Have you won the battle against yourself with clearer thoughts, a stronger consciousness and insight after abstaining from what we devour so routinely?

How about a digital diet?

No TV, e-mail, computer, mobile phone for say 5 days? You don't think so? Have you tried it? Who is to tell you what's good and what's not?

Getting started

A new game, a new chance! The mountain in front of you seems huge, but with each step you get closer to the top. Don't give up. Desire it and follow through. That's the plan.

The reward waits at the end and not at the beginning. No more talking about how you are too old, it is too late, you have no time, no money, etc.

Think about it, if you only had half a year left! How fast would you live, think, feel and absorb everything?

Recognize everything, cold or warm, important or unimportant, then finally set priorities about what still fits into your life and what garbage and distractions you can give up.

All or nothing! You are still alive!

Yes, sometimes you have to say with with brutal honesty.

This is not a dress rehearsal. You're already in the middle of the rest of your life.

The clock is ticking and you have to take the wheel of your life in your hand to be able to say "I did it!" at the end.

Yes, at the top of your lungs. Not regretting anything and being able to say to yourself: "Yes, I've lived!"

Will my book only become a bestseller when I am dead?

Anyway, the message was always bigger than me. If you helped just one person, your life was worth living.

But don't wait to join the orchestra until the conductor says so. Be proactive yourself and set a good example. Do it for yourself and do it for others.

The main thing is that you do it!

We often glorify our past when we were still beautiful and full of energy. The good old days. Today everything is so much different and worse.

A wise man once told me:

Yesterday is gone and doesn't give you one dollar!

Yes, yesterday is gone and I hope you enjoyed it. But today is now!

What are you doing today? Dusting off awards and trophies from yesterday or making a plan for tomorrow? Don't waste your time with sentimentalities from yesterday.

You are a different person today with different priorities. You are now living with a different body, mind and soul. Accept it and you will successfully continue your journey.

Look forward, not back. You can of course enjoy the great things of your past again from your inner eye and bring them back to your memory, but think about tomorrow while you are 100% here today and consciously experience and enjoy the moment.

What remains of the past? Wistful memories of a better world? Was it really so great and beautiful?

Maybe only because it is over now and it no longer hurts and brings harm.

Yes, back then... The good old times...

But you know it's an illusion and we remember only as it suits us. You don't remember days, months, years. You only remember certain moments.

So you make room in the here and now for new, exciting moments. Be here now with all your life experiences.

More courageous and determined. Your life will then give you what you deserve.

Those who accept the circumstances should not be surprised if nothing more exciting happens. As young people, were we interested in the worries and needs of our parents?

Didn't the descendants and the younger generation also have their way of thinking? That has always been the case. That's not important.

What matters is how you shape your morning today and where your place in life is.

New generations have new answers to things we see differently. In the end, we know that we all follow the same path, i.e. life, and each one hopes to master it better than the others.

The question is and remains: How much will you commit to changing what you want to change?

Awareness

All the quick gratifications such as food, alcohol and sex cause a temporary feeling of happiness. In the long run we want to find meaning in life. Does one have to be slightly crazy to achieve this?

Certainly not, but a great passion and curiosity should already be present to experience this happiness I call "the adventure of life" and to fill it with exciting moments.

Being positive is okay, but don't complain later that it's already over while you were still waiting for everything from the outside.

As I said, all happiness comes from within and you have to be able to bear it well in order to move along on your path of life.

Wherever you are and whatever you are doing right now, do it from now on with full awareness and with feeling.

Nothing is stronger than the passion for things you love and appreciate. No explanations, no justifications. Just be and do it.

Enjoy life from sunrise to sunset. How much is in between?

No more putting off anything until tomorrow. Instead experience everything in the here and now. This is the formula for your new life. Don't wait, but experience and enjoy the present moment. That's what it's all about.

Letting go, getting involved and allowing it. That sounds so simple and it is.

Have you ever tried it?

Because it is your life, I would say give it a try. In the end you will discover it is a lot of fun.

We often lie to ourselves and justifying has never been a good choice.

So full speed ahead toward life. More adventure and more experiences out there in the jungle of life to feel centered again.

Of course, sometimes it's all too much. What do you mean by "sometimes?"

Actually, we are always overwhelmed and it is all too much for us. Too many appointments, too many choices, too little focus.

What else can and should we do?

Is "doing more" the answer?

Multiply your success and accordingly multiply your income.

Nobody tells you what price you will ultimately pay for it. Pausing on the highway of life is not desirable or appropriate.

Self-determination

Here we go again!

Who will call the shots, if not you?

Try something new. Take the plunge. Don't just be creative on vacation when you want to change everything once a year and get off the treadmill of your life.

We take ourselves everywhere with us, even to the ends of the Earth.

You should make peace with yourself on the inside and then radiate to the outside what is really important to you.

The island can help you to realize what you no longer want and what you really want.

Then you have to act and realize your dreams.

Who else has so many possibilities and chances as we have today? Surely it cannot be that we are constantly paying for not reaching our dreams with excuses. Life is not about we would have or could have done.

We would have done it by now if it wasn't working because…

You need more time…

You need more money…

We'll have to rethink that.

Go for it!

Life is always "Now!"

Later might be too late!

Adventure or burden? Relax or burden?

Our view of things is crucial. We have a body, a mind and a soul. Are these really units or does everyone do their thing?

What percentage of life are we living?

When do we want to live our potential?

Why don't we make this agreement with ourselves? What really hinders us and what is our greatest fear? Failure – failure?

What will other people think?

What is really holding us back?

Animals don't think. They follow their instincts. Isn't it time we listen to our instincts again?

The golden thread that supposedly runs through our lives.

How often do we not see it? Do we see it at all?

Life plan

Here too the question arises:

Do we have a plan – a life plan? Does something simply happen every day?

If you are happy with what you have, that is wonderful. To think that it will always be like this would be very naive.

No expectations, no disappointments. That's right, but still we always want more and go to our limits.

There's more? Anything new? Something else?

Life is constantly changing and we too are different today than we were ten years ago.

"Go with the flow."

Yes, find out what really inspires and motivates you. A new hobby, painting, writing, photography, sports, nutrition, new love, new passion?

Whatever it is, it's up to you to live your life to the fullest and be the creator of what you do. Listen to the stories of people who view life as a gift.

All the adventures and human tragedies that show us how vulnerable we are and yet what each and every one of us can achieve when we accept the challenges of life and ride on its wave.

It's all so close together:

> – Success and failure.
> – Good luck and bad luck.
> – Health and illness.
> – Sunshine and rain.

We know about Yin and Yang and that light and shadow are two sides of the same coin.

We just want the sunny side of life, but then suddenly everything changes.

A stroke of fate, a loss, an imbalance, when we would like to have everything always under control. So what are the rules of life?

Philosophers have racked their brains over this for thousands of years. From Seneca to Stephen Hawking, everyone has expressed their opinions.

It's time for you to give answers to your own life and be grateful for it.

Your contribution

What is your contribution in life and what do you want people to say about you when you are no longer here?

Because then it will be too late to intervene in the events!

Therefore, let us try to do here and now everything that is really important to us and then act accordingly.

Turn another page in your book of life before you go to bed.

Get up again to find out what you really want. So many things to do, so many things to consider, and yet you must steer the ship of your life.

What has happened to humanity?

What's the point of having children?

Your own life runs daily and hopefully not just once. Comparing and seeing what others do is legitimate and can be done.

What does it benefit and help you for your life? To give?

Striving for higher things?

Why not?

You only have this one life, no matter what you do. Your mind, body and soul will never rest.

So start small but begin somehow so no one can ever escape your cause.

People don't laugh anymore because they're not happy. It takes alcohol and other things to feel. But be different and go your own way. It's already too late for many.

But then all of a sudden there is the miracle.

Yes, our friend with cancer got an "all clear" on his last scan. After nine rounds of chemotherapy, there's no tumor left after months of struggle, hope and despair.

He lost 20 kilos of weight, no food, and vomiting after chemo. Now the miracle! The fatal tumor is gone, however. Now it's time to reevaluate, experience and feel the life that was renewed. Once again, we have jumped off death's bandwagon. For how long? It doesn't matter because from now on every moment counts. To understand and realize it is the art of life.

"I am still alive and for everything there is a price."

People who were believed to have died live longer and in any case more intensely. We don't have to go that far, but we are shown the finiteness of life again.

Where is our void?

Where can we fill that deficit?

Certainly not if external forces drive our lives instead of our living it ourselves.

"Enjoy life and life will give back to you."

Will to live

It slowly returns: our power, our energy, our will to live.

Living more consciously, being more attentive, eating better, communicating better and showing that we care, for ourselves and for others.

To enjoy life together and to master the challenges together.

So much has been written about life planning and time management. Even with really simple tips you can change your life for the long term.

Take a 30-minute walk in the fresh air every day. 15 minutes of mediation every day.

Engage in dinner cancellation twice a week. No eating after 6 pm and work on three things a day towards your goals.

For example, if you want to write a book, you could work on three things:

1. Send the manuscript to publishers.
2. Send a press release to radio stations.
3. Talk with other authors and writers.

If you do three things a day toward your goal, you will come closer and closer to reaching it.

I also mentioned that getting up an hour earlier, especially in the summer months, can increase your productivity by 10-20%.

So just be creative in creating your day. There is no perfect moment to start!

Every new week can be reason enough to reschedule your day and set new priorities.

It should be fun and you get an overview of what you are up to and have already achieved.

While setting your goals and daily tasks, you realize more and more that you are the creator of your life.

The challenges become more manageable and your sense of achievement grows. With planning and a somewhat strategic approach, you have tools at hand to help you carry out your tasks.

This way you can always work on several projects at the same time and still never lose sight of the big goal.

You decide yourself which workload you want to work on every day. Even small steps will lead you to great deeds in the end. It does not depend on how fast you go; it depends on the fact that you go at all.

Keep moving and stay flexible. Enjoy the journey and learn every day, like in the sea.

Wave upon wave and everything moves. Create your own flow. Get feedback from people you know and appreciate.

Your planner becomes your companion through daily life and accompanies you in all your projects.

What can you build into your life every day that give you joy and the feeling of being productive?

Thus, your sense of achievement starts in the little things and accompanies you from smaller to bigger goals with more and more visible success.

It will become your new habit to write in your life-journal, adding in your secrets much like a diary, which is only meant for you.

A constant, faithful companion, waiting to be filled with your ideas and plans.

Thus, you create the conditions for your very first book, filled with the stories of your life and impressions and adventures that want to be told.

You already have a new hobby and are in constant dialogue with yourself.

You have something to say? Then say it!

Your program

Design your own program and reduce external media consumption.

Everything is present within you. Let it out and bring it to life.

When intuition and planning go hand in hand, you will achieve great things and you will be given the satisfaction you seek to live your inner happiness.

If you then have the right life partner at your side, your life can become perfect.

Live what makes you happy.

Listen to your favorite music. Sing and dance to your life rhythm. You will become master of your own universe and soon the world will revolve around you.

Start to communicate, visualize and realize your dreams.

From now on nobody can stop you.

You want to learn, write your deepest thoughts in your journal and discover new things. Now you are hot and there is no going back into a world where you have lived in this way.

Now you have the rudder in your hand and are waiting with joy for the next exciting day. You know that you can create and change it.

On to new horizons!

On to new adventures!

Suddenly you are right in the middle of it and that is the purpose. The meaning of life!

Not just half, but full!

Let go of the past and do not think about what will be or could be. Giving your all now and only now while silencing everything sounds easy and it is.

However, we were always too busy to know this truth. So what made us open up? Does it always have to be a blow of fate or can't it be done with your inner voice and intuition?

It always works if you allow it and listen to it. You also have a guardian angel, but do you really want to hear that? He is not well because he is always there for you and you believe in him only conditionally, if at all?

There is always more there than we believe and can imagine. A three-dimensional life! There is certainly more. Do we stay in the here and now? What do you want to change? What can you change and what must you change?

It's up to you to answer these questions and to make the right decisions. You have procrastinated long enough. Now it is time to act. A life in the now.

When we listen to the news, we know how many terrible things can happen in a week.

The holy week before Easter 2019 for Christians, for example. The roof of the 850-year-old cathedral Notre Dame in Paris collapsed in a fire and days later an attack in Sri Lanka on three hotels and three churches with 215 dead and 500 injured occurred.

All fate? Individual fates? Do we look away or do we look toward things? How can we contribute, what can we change?

Awareness

It starts with being attentive and realizing the things that are happening around us. We move from taking things for granted, criticizing and judging toward gratitude and humility. There are so many things we cannot and never will understand; however, starting on a small scale, being human is always a good option. You may not be able to prevent the "worst case scenario", but you can contribute so many positive things to this world with your attitude and your lived example.

Sinking into depression and telling yourself, What can I do? is not an option at the start.

A positive or negative thought needs the same energy. But the result is 100% different.

Look at the bright side of life and approach everything with humor.

Think "It's all just a movie" and you will shape the result.

Be your best friend, because as I said, you have to endure 24 hours every day with yourself. This can be a lot easier when you apply humor and fun.

If you like comics, comedy or Mr. Bean, you may laugh at their weird behavior.

Don't take yourself or life too seriously. There is so much outside of us as well as within us that we will never fully understand life itself.

Live with the flow and let it go!

People hardly read books any more. I joyfully gave away the first book I wrote and dedicated it to people.

There was not a lot of good feedback. One person even said: "I think I will wait for the movie!"

So whenever you think of doing something for others, think of yourself and what is important to you.

Some people will be inspired and they will really help you. Others will have expected something else. *Yes, I imagined it differently, sorry*!

What do your critics do? Do they go out and try it themselves? Certainly not, certainly never!

To have an opinion and to criticize is so much easier. You get rid of a lot. If you want to be your best friend, you often have to satisfy yourself and not wait and hope for the praise of others.

Artists usually become famous only after their death. Nevertheless, be the artist of your life and don't wait in vain for recognition from outside.

When the fire burns within you, you are setting a trend somewhere. If the success comes, everything was right; if not, the project is null and void.

But also here others should not decide about your success. You should always remain true to yourself. What is right today may be wrong tomorrow. It is a question of perception. If it feels good for you, it is right.

There is a power that can become a collective when you are in contact with other people who guide you on your path in a positive way and try to understand what you want to express.

Jesus already said: Where two are united in my name, I am among them!

Brainstorming together helps so much. It can give you a push the direction you are taking with energy and willpower and the feedback you receive is essential.

What's missing?

What is really missing to reach your goals?

Money?
Time?
ideas?

Stick with it and go your way every day. You will be surprised how far you can get in a short time. Setbacks and discouragement are normal and if it were easy, everyone would achieve their goals automatically.

The successful one keeps on going and the unsuccessful one gives up after a few setbacks.

What would be different if you only had one year to live?

Your priorities and actions would definitely look different.

Don't wait until you have no more time. Take the 24 hours that exist every day only if God wills it.

In an effort to help you use your life time more powerfully, I want to offer you a few modules to get you closer to reaching your daily and life goals, much like a workbook.

Workout

Let us begin with module 1:

Workout for a successful life:

Two things are important here:

Awareness and action.

How you start your day is how it will unfold. So start consciously.

When you open your eyes, be grateful that you are still here.

Go to the window. Open it and breathe in and out consciously for one minute. Then stretch and do some exercise.

Then you can either go to the bathroom and get ready for the day, brush your teeth, take a shower etc. or have breakfast first.

Very important: Think for a minute about which five things you absolutely want to do today to get closer to your goals.

Don't start turning on your mobile phone and computer right away.

Switch yourself on first and get your body, mind and soul in motion and at operating speed.

Perhaps you might go to the bakery. Do everything consciously and with joy.

A new day lies before you. Design it according to your own thoughts.

How do you get to work?

By car, by train, by metro, by bike or on foot?

Do you work from home?

Which route to work do you take?

At what time of day?

Do you have superiors, colleagues or employees?

You cannot *not* work!

So make a good impression everywhere. Make sure you eat the right food and above all drink enough water.

Now to the topic: Check your e-mail.

Most senders want something from you and often make it important or urgent.

Here is the most important question to yourself: How important or urgent is this to me?

Set priorities and also communicate that you only answer e-mails once or three times a day.

With the multitude of e-mail that we all write every day, you could write a book and put your thoughts about the world in writing.

Don't let others stress you out unnecessarily and remember: Sometimes it starts with a harmless e-mail and then we get into a wild back-and-forth correspondence.

This is not what you want!

Break time

On to module 2:

Coffee or lunch break

Breaks are important and become valuable if you decide beforehand when to take a break and with whom.

Which conversation do you want to have during the break? What kind of food and beverage do you want to drink?

Breaks are there to regenerate. Perhaps a short walk would be useful.

Breathe in and out consciously. Can you close your eyes for 10-20 minutes? Do a meditation or take a little nap.

Consciously gather strength for the second half of the day.

Don't toss back one coffee after the other. Push yourself mentally with things that really interest you.

Avoid gossip and don't blab about superiors, colleagues or others. That won't get you anywhere.

Your body, mind and soul are a divine vessel. Be careful what you put into it.

You give your car the best gasoline. You shouldgive yourself the best too because you deserve it.

It is so important what kind of thoughts you have because your thoughts create your reality.

Stay away from negative people and negative thoughts. Try to live your life with joy and reward yourself when you have achieved what you wanted.

Trust yourself a little bit more every day and enjoy the time you consciously spend with yourself every day.

Your inner voice will then come out regularly and you will get a feeling for what is good for you and what is not.

Listen to your inner soul!

For this you should also stretch yourself a little bit. Be an adventurer again and try something new every day.

For example: Get up an hour earlier than usual during the summer and enjoy the day before it gets light outside.

Be grateful, meditate or go for a 30-minute walk. Do some sports or read 30 pages. Write or take pictures of the sunrise.

Consciously dedicate time with yourself to recognize who you are and feel good about yourself.

Your master plan:

The year is half over and you have that all too familiar feeling that you are once again behind on your goals?

Change your point of view. Make sure you have six months left for this year to reach your goals. Get started!

Every book you write has 365 pages if you write just one page a day. Within six months, you could have 180 pages, which is more than most books have on average these days.

Take off the pressure and step into action, just like in sports. When you do your first pushups, you might do 5-10. With practice, you can get increase your performance very quickly.

Free your mind! Off you go!

Don't focus on the burden, but on the joy and the creative momentum.

You can do what you enjoy in so many different places and you have the technique to communicate from almost any-where in the world.

Use your sources and enjoy your life daily because it is the greatest gift we have.

Become an explorer and adventurer again and have a vision for today and tomorrow.

It's like dawn. At first you only see outlines and shadows. As it slowly gets brighter, you see the picture more clearly.

You see the whole picture and can choose where you want to go. Enjoy this freedom and immerse yourself in the picture you have created. You are the creator of your life and nobody else.

But you need a plan. It is not the size that matters, but whatever you plan to do, work on its implementation. No matter how small the steps are, look towards your goal. Always live in the awareness so that you never lose sight of your goal.

It is not about speed, but about consistency. Like a tree, if you hit the same notch often enough, it will fall down one day.

Every day there are another 24 hours for you, if God wills it. So be productive and proactive. Create something every day. A year from now you will be amazed at what you will have achieved.

Can you remember where you were a year ago? Do you see what you have achieved from there until today?

You might not have imagined a lot. Today it seems normal and natural to you.

You have walked a little bit every day on your way and you feel the power that is within you to achieve so much more.

You have so many things you still want to do and achieve. Where do you start?

Step by step!

With a plan!

Three things every day

Consistently write down at least three things that you want and will do every day to achieve your long-term goal.

It is a great feeling to see that only three things you do every day can bring such great results. Enough of all that procrastination and our daily excuses to get things done and bring them to an end.

Set aside a block of time for your productivity. That can be early morning or whenever you are at your best during the day.

Don't let anything distract you such as your mobile phone, etc. Go for it!

Just one hour without distraction while you work on your goal can bring extraordinary results.

Reward yourself afterwards with a shower, an espresso or a short meditation. Stay alert and then get into action. It starts to flow and bring joy.

What do you want to achieve and above all why, by when and who can help you?

Brainstorm who is available in your private and professional network to help you reach your goals.

There is always someone you don" have on your list today. But if your dream is big enough, there is also someone who would like to join you and help you.

Be communicative and tell the world what you have in mind and what you need. You will attract things like a magnet that you did not think possible.

Open your mind to miracles and events that will amaze you. Be the master of your universe and play role of creator. May the adventure begin!

When the first positive habits have been found, e.g. writing three pages a day, spending thirty minutes in nature or not eating twice a week after 6 pm, you will gain confidence in your body, mind and soul.

The crucial thing is that you realize that you are the creator of your day, week, month, year and life.

Now all at once everything makes sense and you become more creative every day and bubble over with energy and ideas. You feel unstoppable and are starting to finally have fun again.

How can you maintain this state of being?

With discipline and a daily routine. The time you plan for yourself is like a date: exciting, thrilling and inspiring.

Put more life into your life and you will get more out of it.

Yes, invest in the most important person there is.

Yourself!

Get to know and appreciate yourself better every day. Be self-centered – that is, centering within yourself – through and through. Try things that are good for you.

Life is a journey to get to know yourself and the sooner you accept this, the sooner you will reach your goals.

We often think that we still have so much time to realize all our dreams and desires.

But every day passes by, whether we have moved toward something or not. Once you get into the "flow," it is as if you are in a trance.

You see how you have limited yourself for so long and that our thinking and brooding are in the way to finally step into action.

Action, not reaction

Get into motion and live in the moment. Don't always judge whether it is good, right or wrong. Just do it and enjoy. You learn something from every situation and that is why we are here.

Always remain curious like a child and to constantly make new experiences that will bring you further towards happiness and the task of life. Move forward while running after some great unknown. Stretching ourselves outside our comfort zone until the unknown becomes known lets us grow. Being brave and standing on our own two feet works wonders.

But then we have self-doubts: Why me?

Who will understand this?

There is so much more that is better and different!

Why should someone pay money for it?

The project is not finished or balanced. It still needs so much content and practice.

Shouldn't we wait just a little while longer?

Later is probably better, then we have prepared everything better.

STOP!

There is no such thing as the perfect time to start. Waiting won't help you. Step on the gas if you can; excuses accompany us all our lives.

Be self-determined and start – at least to live! Say yes to yourself and let it happen.

What do you have to lose apart from your little earthly life?

Start now and you will see that everything is in motion, much of which is moving in your direction. Say yes to your journey and to yourself.

What lies ahead of you? Why does it seem so far and unattainable? What tools are there to get closer to your goals and desires? Take baby steps, but walk, without excuses and interruptions.

Write one page every day and within six months every book you start will be finished!

But there is always a reason why today is not possible. But that's only because we let it. If we are focused and it is important enough to us, we can do what we set out to do. Always having the plan and the goal in mind and making it our task to implement something every day.

Three things a day and in the long run, that habit changes everything. With a little courage and trust to overcome your anxiety daily – to do something towards your future and to be creator of your life and circumstances again.

Sit in the front seat and not in the back! Don't just look ahead and wait. We tend to wait too long for better circumstances and situations in life.

Taking the lead ourselves and proactively shaping each day is the main task; it is worth living for.

Always give your best and be a role model, then we will achieve the necessary discipline. That is where PATIENCE is at the forefront.

Of course, you want to start running right away, feeling your energy and wanting to get into action. Most of the time, however, it is better to be patient and approach things with care and clarity.

It is not about speed. It is about moving in the right direction. Every step in the right direction takes us forward. Every kilometer that is driven too fast will make us correct our course.

If you know your rhythm, you can always be more productive.

If you keep your energy high, ask yourself: are you most energetic in the morning, at noon, in the afternoon or in the evening?

It is better to get up an hour earlier in the morning and have already put a lot into action than to get up too late and spend the whole day running after lost time.

Always keep the three most important daily goals in sight and work step by step on their implementation. Do the most annoying things of the day first.

You have to deal with it.

When you overcome unpleasant tasks, the things that bring joy will come. Every step gives you the feeling that you have not shortchanged yourself, but that you have really done it.

You determine the speed and also when and where you are most productive. Making it a habit to do something is the plan.

One page every day and in six months the rough draft of a book is ready. 180 pages!

Now comes the proofreading, editing, cover and branding. You should have the title right from the start. Talk to the right people and off you go.

What is holding you back?

Be playful and adventuresome. Don't try to be too perfect. Just do it. What do you have to lose?

Have the ending in your head at the beginning. Visualize your project and imagine how others congratulate you for your great work.

Do a little magic and live your dream a little more every day.

Here is something magical:

Yes, you heard that right. Listen! Let the other person speak first, wait until he is done and then continue with your own thoughts. Let others finish their sentences and concentrate on listening without reacting right away and stating your opinion.

This act of empathy is what will change your life. Showing interest in life and other people's stories will make a difference. No one seems to have time anymore for anyone and the stories they need to tell.

People are so preoccupied with their own concerns and it seems so very important how our own lives are unfolding. But everything and everyone is connected and the sooner we accept and understand that, the more we can become active and interact with life.

Genuine compassion is one of the greatest things you can give to a living being. Even plants notice how real and honest you are. Try it out.

Be patient and listen. A spark of love will come over you and make your heart swell.

That productivity improves and increases if you keep at it seems only too logical.

As in any discipline, be it sports or a profession, the more we practice, the better we get at it. The 10,000 hours of Malcolm Gladwell's work leading to perfection in each discipline is an indicator of what can be achieved if you make it your life's work be centered on becoming the best in your field.

But as I said, if God wills, there are 24 new hours a day that we can use meaningfully to achieve our life goals.

The beginning is difficult and what is even more difficult is to keep it up. Discipline, patience and perseverance are needed here.

To overcome oneself daily and even to go the extra mile for one's cause seems difficult or even impossible. Nevertheless, this is what we fill our time with. If we grant power to too many external distractions that scatter our thoughts, then we only run from A to B and back again.

Like a tree. If the axe always hits the same notch, even the biggest tree will fall one day. Always stay focused on the end result, even if it is often far away.

Like when you start tennis tomorrow. The first stroke may seem ridiculous, but with every further stroke you can only get better. Don't forget your sense of humor. Doggedness is counterproductive and never gets anyone anywhere.

Think of Mr. Bean or the Simpsons. How they stumble from one situation to another and end up doing so much.

Walking, not stopping is the motto and every now and then stop and look where you are. Trying to do too many tasks at once brings nothing but frustration.

If you reach your daily goals, even if there are only three, you will also reach your weekly, monthly and annual goals.

Speak with your inner voice and let your creator come alive within you. It is all there; it just needs to be used.

Finding some supporters for your project, be it mentally, financially or as a feedback provider, will help you stay motivated to deliver within the agreed time frame.

Being able to act self-determined is a great gift and helps you express your individuality.

How terrible would it be if you didn't have the courage and ambition to pull yourself together and present the things that are lying dormant within you to the world?

We only have this one life and even if we are reborn many times, it is the here and now that counts. This is the challenge we should all face.

Self-doubts

In the end, it is always our own doubts that prevent us from taking giant steps with our heads held high with joy and confidence in realizing our dreams. We do not have to envy anyone who is younger or has any other qualities we might desire.

They too have talents that should be used and made visible.

The reward waits at the end of the journey and not at its beginning. Only when we do it do we realize what we are capable of.

When the bridges under you are burned, there is only one way forward and only one goal to make it. To have never tried it is shameful. Everything else belongs to life, even the small and bigger setbacks.

The commitment and the dedication to your own cause is the decisive momentum.

If you have made this promise to yourself, you will try everything not to disappoint yourself and the world.

We live in a time where all resources are available 24 hours a day.

Help yourself in the supermarket of life and have fun when you see that seemingly impossible things become possible at once.

The hero accepts the challenges and solves task after task. Gather active spiritual allies along your path. Ask for help if you need it.

People will be happy to support you and help you because people love it when someone has the courage to break out of the comfort zone and journey into the unknown.

Our life is a journey and ultimately a journey toward ourselves, but on this path many companions will accompany us and help us reach our goal.

It is never just about ourselves, but always about everyone. We are one human species and we all learn from each other. If we act in a humane manner, we will have understood what this planet is all about.

Many billions of people were on this planet before us, but not all of them have realized their dreams and desires.

Let those who have made their dreams come true be an example for us to never give up on this journey together. You too will be guided, if you allow it and activate the power within you.

There is so much energy waiting to be transformed into something new and creative.

Maybe you get a little bit frightened when you realize that you are actually about to be the creator of your life or when a few new habits suddenly make things happen that you thought impossible not so long ago. Or when your body and mind suddenly swing in harmony and the soul also makes itself felt and your senses are sharpened, your attention increased in such a way that you perceive things that were previously nonexistent.

If you still have a desire to take action and provide pleasure and goodness to others, then it is obvious that you are on the right path.

However, again and again we get distracted, held up, kept short and lose the drive to complete the projects we have set out to do.

But with every page more in the book, with every additional action in life we will move in the right direction towards a fulfilled life that has purpose and provides meaning!

Just keep going and focus on the final goal. Everything can be over tomorrow and there are no guarantees for anything.

But once again:

What counts most is that you have tried.

If we don't dare to do it, we will always regret what we have missed. The struggle within ourselves is the biggest and the most exciting when we take on those challenges.

Don't always ask, what will I get out of it? What advantage will I have? In every cave there's a dragon and with every battle you become stronger.

Finding friends and allies along the way makes things easier and provides you with the right feedback.

But in the end, you have to make the decision on your own.

It's your life, now or never, paraphrased from a song by Bon Jovi. It is the greatest motto for life ever.

It shouldn't happen just like that. We should lead and direct. With courage, strength and confidence, then the obstacle also disappears.

Try it out. A bit every day because this day right now will soon be gone.

Here and now and right in the middle of it, then you will feel life. Then it makes sense!

Pause – Mediation – Reflection

Review the steps you have taken and the decisions you have made. Pause and listen to your inner voice.

What have you been dreaming lately? Do you get in touch with your higher self and listen to your inner child?

Many signals and signs are constantly there to strengthen you.

There is more out there than we think, but oftentimes we only want to trust reason. When you are in love, you are simply happy and do not know exactly why.

Allow feelings and thoughts that sometimes don't fit into our everyday lives.

Leave the frame sometimes. Create something new with your thoughts. Dream during the day and allow yourself to try out new things. New people, impressions, statements, countries, philosophers, expand in new terrain and be curious like a child.

Don't close your eyes anymore and be amazed at what there is. Life is a buffet and you have to take what is good for you.

What helps is to read the biographies of the people you admire.

Today there are podcasts and so much info on all the topics that interest you. If you want to follow a path, there is and always has been someone who has done so before you.

You can orientate yourself by the steps of those who have walked that path or are currently walking it. We are not alone in the universe. It is all there. It only needs a plan to implement and the courage to start.

Even if the doubts start to creep up again, ignore what you think is not possible and keep trying and practicing. Experiencing embarrassment is not all that bad and, quite honestly, people are too preoccupied with themselves to notice. By tomorrow, that embarrassment will have been forgotten.

But for our own success we have to believe in ourselves and fight. Doing nothing brings us nothing. Neither does it help to wait. Moving towards the goal is the motto.

Go for it!

Small successes show us what is possible on a large scale. Keep at it even if you don't feel able to bring it to a good end at all.

Continue even on those days when every fiber of your being in you says: Quit! It's no use. Who's going to want to read and listen to it or even like it?

Yes, it's a lonely job and yet it's worth walking every foot of the way. To go further. To go on without guarantees of what will ever come of it. To have the courage not to give up and leave a message that can help so many people understand that we all have our problems and we are not alone, even if we often feel that way.

Edit that sentence once again, try to be clearer, try to knock everything over again and try to get it into a better shape; yes, that's the walk of life. Every day we get a new opportunity to move things in the right direction.

Excuses never help us and if we believe in one thing, it will succeed.

In this day and age, we have access to so many tools and sources of information. From Google to Wikipedia. The Internet, YouTube, tutorials and amazon have so many capabilities for everyone to access. It's fun to pick one thing and work on it.

So much preliminary work has already been done. We just have to get it right. There is no perfect moment to start.

Today is better than tomorrow and if you stick with it, you can do more in a year than you ever dreamed possible.

Every day provides new opportunities to make your dreams come true.

So, here we go:

"Do Something!" "Do It Now!"

If you knew that no matter what you do, you couldn't possibly fail, what would you do?

So try it, even without the net and the false bottom.

The only way is up! So what? Try it!

At this point I would like to tell you a true story from the year 1914:

One of the most famous inventors in the history of the world, Thomas Alva Edison, watched ten of his buildings burn to the ground in a huge fire. Only a third of the damage was paid for by insurance. Worse than that, all his priceless notes and prototypes were destroyed.

What did Edison do? He told his 24-year-old son, "Go get Mom. Everything's fine. All our mistakes are burning up there and we can start all over again!"

A little later he told a New York Times reporter, "I may be 67 years old, but I'll start fresh tomorrow."

And that is exactly what he did. The very next morning he got started. Edison borrowed money from his friend Henry Ford, had the workshop repaired and achieved record sales of 10 million dollars the very next year.

A very young intelligent event manager recently asked me which book I would take with me if my apartment burned down and I could only rescue one book from my library.

Wow, finally a question that makes you think! Then I thought about it and answered immediately: "It would be the book *Success Principles* by Jack Canfield."

He is not only my role model, mentor and friend, but I was also allowed to be a co-author and co-producer of his life's work *Soul of Success* in book and film form!

Whoever applies the wisdom in *Success Principles* will have 100% success in his life. With his book series *Chicken Soup for the Soul*, Jack Canfield proved that it is possible to move hundreds of millions of people by his touching true stories.

Role model

Find a role model and make contact. You will never know what is possible if you are not open to the extraordinary.

There is no such thing as coincidence. Your life leads you to your goal. Be ready for great things.

You know, it's like an iceberg.

Only 10% of it sticks out of the water and is visible. 90% of it is underwater. It's like your subconscious mind. If we are always satisfied with only 10% of what is visible, we will never know what the adventure of life has hidden for us.

Sharpen your consciousness, be open and try out new things. That is the thing we should get involved in. The same thing over and over again. Out of habit, out of security, the known, the predictable – really?

Then suddenly everything changes.

One moment can change your life.

I spent two and a half years writing a book by that title, interviewing people young and old on the subject. What was your moment that changed your life positively or negatively forever?

You meet the love of your life on a train platform. You get a job offer and go abroad for 10 years.

A near-death experience. A divorce. The loss of a loved one. Everything can be different in an instant.

Michael Schuhmacher, Lady Di, Christopher Reeves, even *Ed Sheeran,* who was still playing music on sidewalks just eight years ago and is now considered one of the top five musicians in the industry.

Anything is possible. If you allow it and believe in yourself and the universe, things will happen that you never thought possible. Focus on your life's dream and if it sounds crazy, do not let yourself be diverted from your own path toward yourself.

Work with fun and joy on the fact that you can be successful at something others think is impossible.

Why you?
Why not?

It is the best time for change. Be brave, go ahead and try it out as if you were still a child. You are a child of the universe and don't stand in your own way because otherwise it really will be too late.

Feel the power within. There is a voice that belongs to you and says so many things. Be open and also ready. There are so many possibilities; do not be afraid. Listen to the voice and feel what is good for you.

Many do not have the opportunity to do this.

If you are fit, you must do it. Be a role model for others and go forward courageously, then the impossible will become possible and you will be a part of it all.

Feel that something is moving and also understand that it is never too late.

But time is an illusion, as Albert Einstein said. Energy never fades and we are all energy.

So we still have enough time to start plans, projects and fulfill dreams within our lifetime. Don't wait and just do it. The ride may be bumpy at first, but then, over time, it will get so much better.

Everything we need is within us all so it is time to express it. It is a challenge for time, but to embrace it will take us far.

Structuring your life plan and being aware of your life's purpose are what takes us forward.

No annoying to-do lists, just the big picture in mind, like the fixed star in the evening sky.

That is the long-term goal.

For every day, week, month and year we need milestones.

Just as every week begins anew on Monday, we should be ready to have our daily and weekly schedule prepared.

What are our priorities and what do we really want to achieve on that day?

To implement three important things daily makes us the *"Master of Life"* in the long run.

Habits

If it is then possible to exchange bad habits for good habits, we will become more and more self-confident and successful. There is only this one life. When we have understood that fact, we will also find the path that suits us best. With every courageous step we approach our goals and desires. Suddenly, our time is perceived as the most precious thing in the world.

Yes, our own lifetime is the most precious thing we have here. Earthly goods are perishable and replaceable. Our lifetime is not. Nevertheless, we do everything to pass the time and allow any distraction, so that we do not become aware that the right handling of our lifetime is the key to happiness, harmony and fulfilment.

If we learn to use our time here on Earth in the right way, then we will succeed in everything. Even if a lot of time has already been wasted, there is still the possibility to use the time that is left to us meaningfully.

The past is over and the future is vague. However, the present – this here and now – is our paradise.

If we succeed in living and enjoying the moment, we will also be able to look back on a fulfilled life. Outside influence is good and we can Google any problem on the Internet, but you have the greatest wonder of all: your inner voice, your intuition and your previous life experience. This is so strong and powerful and is, as with Aladdin, a genie in a bottle, which is available to you at any time, if you know and follow the formula of life.

Inside and outside. The whole universe is within us and we just have to get in contact with our base station again. For this you need trust in yourself.

It is all there in our world. Coaches, seminars etc. But it is also all within you.

It only needs to be recognized and activated. Your so-called "calling" leads you down the right path, but you have to go for it yourself.

But it is help and support on that path. It is said, "When the student is ready, the teacher appears."

Now it is time to find the right teacher for you, your mentor and spirit who touches you with all his ideas and leads you through all the jungle of possibilities to find the right path for yourself.

This can take a long time, even years. It is like a distant expedition. In the end you understand that you have taken yourself along everywhere and in the end none of us can escape our life's work.

How much better it is when we realize that we should not miss any time to set out on our way toward ourselves. Always excuses, always distraction.

No, if you make that the number one priority in your life, nothing else will matter.

You gain so much more self-respect because you get to keep your promise.

How proud you will be be if you follow your diet or abstain from alcohol for a longer period of time or if you do sports!

Your own overcoming gives you strength for more.

It is as always. As soon as you have mobilized yourself and entered into action, everything is different.

We are talking about flow, the feeling of happiness, the serotonin release while jogging.

No, going your own way and staying with it, without knowing what is and will be, is the confirmation of having felt and known that the reward is waiting and being handed over at the end of the journey.

Most others have long since given up and retreated to their comfort zone with explanations and excuses about why things didn't work out.

But as a winner, you are not interested in that. Everything seems absurd and everything is strange, but you think and know that it is still the right path.

A lot of things seem to be in vain and for naught and you never know beforehand if all the effort will have been worth it.

Nevertheless, following your inner voice is what will be rewarded if you persevere with what we stand for.

What is it that really triggers us and why?

What is your why?

What do we want to change, achieve, move and leave behind in this world?

Our ego or really sensible things? Who sets the bar and for what and why?

Sometimes we become humble, grateful and don't care.

We have a plan. We have a life. Then things turn out differently and a lot of things go wrong and still we keep on fighting. We are not stupid.

The big thing, the thing itself, is what we want to get right. Time goes on and every day it becomes clear to us what needs to be done.

Your mindset, attitude and that simple feeling "out there." There is so much we don't understand yet and we all hope we can survive and live as long as we like.

Then fate enters the room and issues around our family, our profession, health and happiness drive us crazy. We want the best and yet we operate the way society wants us to.

The feeling to change ourselves, the courage for something new and everything from today and without regret.

How far do I go, what do I say? We often get too lonely and fall into a black hole. The fear is bigger and the victory smaller, but everything is in upheaval and we are at war with ourselves.

We don't want to see it and yet everything is right before our very eyes. A day without suffering is wonderful.

Looking toward instead of looking away. That's what we should do. We'll never rest in peace in the face of all that looking away.

It concerns all of us and time is running out. To have at least tried calms us in our graves. Be a hero and step on it!

Everything else is true and who benefits from it?

No, as we all know, the smallest steps help and sometimes it's just a kick in the backside. The main thing is movement and that is where it all starts in the end.

The cycle of life repeats itself so often, but we think it is all just new again.

The most important thing is:

Stay true to yourself!

No analysis and no protocol tell you what you really need to know. Do it alone and believe in yourself. In the end you are smarter and everyone else is crazy.

We all have the potential to make things happen, but our motivation to do so is drowned out by so many excuses. We keep getting held up by ourselves. To break through this hesitation and action is the highest bidding to achieve our goals.

Doing things that make you feel uncomfortable because you don't know what the end result will be is essential for us to be able love ourselves and to grow, once you leave familiar ground. Like in nature, it is about either growing or stagnating.

The fear of failure is normal. Having the courage to do it anyway makes us successful and self-confident.

It is like sports. Through constant practice we achieve results that initially seemed impossible. To see your life as an adventure and to live it is the greatest challenge there is. There is not too little time available; we just don't use it properly.

The courage to stand up for yourself and to realize your dreams and desires lets us mature to become the greatest version of ourselves. Our environment senses how self-confident we are. But then to keep at it and never give up again, this is the time to live for.

"Be the best version of yourself"

becomes the motto of life.

Continuously working on being and giving our "very best" allows us to achieve and endure anything. We have to go through the process of life anyway, so why not as heroes?

Focusing on the opportunity every day to implement something within 24 hours is a lot. Certainly, there are always doubts and fears and you always want to question whether it is worth it or not.

Just get started. Paint a picture or speak your first own podcast into your mobile phone.

We love children who invent something new every day and playfully shape their own lives.

We too are big kids who should just get started without questioning everything. We are the creators of our lives and we have a right to use our remaining lifetime to do things that bring us fun and joy.

It will just get worse on its own. We have to do something for our happiness and well-being. If you want to dream, then dream big!

Our thoughts determine our actions. If you concentrate on strollers, you will suddenly see lots of strollers.

Our brain is a muscle to be trained. Visualization and imagination help us to make our goals and desires imaginable and if you put enough energy into it, the necessary power to realize these goals and desires is created.

You have nothing to lose; you can only win. Try it out. Every day, even if only for 20 minutes: Close your eyes and dream your dream life!

You will love this experiment and nobody knows your secret. Things will happen that you never thought possible.

The greatest power lies within us and you have a lifetime to discover this treasure and use it for yourself and the world.

Everything you want to have on the outside must first be created on the inside.

Like an architect who first has an idea and then puts it down on paper and draws up a feasible plan. Be the architect of your life and don't let anyone talk you out of your dreams.

You have a right to your own life and you can always start something new and try it out.

At any moment everything can change, positive or negative.

Try to anticipate things that are in a state of upheaval with great attention.

You have your Aladdin within you. Your inner voice never leaves you. Talk to it. Ask it. Trust it and listen to it.

Intuition becomes stronger if you trust and follow your inner feelings.

Drifting away from the mainstream and then following our own path brings the fulfillment we all seek, which requires courage and faith. You have the power to do it. Only doubts and fears keep us from the big goals and dreams.

You have nothing to lose but your life and we all lose that in the end! So, as long as we can still make a difference, let us make a contribution and leave something of importance to the world.

Giving meaning to your own life, helping others to find their meaning, being human and living a self-confident life in community with others is what is required to be happy.

There is no signpost for life, but there are tried and true methods that make it easier for you to exist and be happy in this increasingly complex world.

There are so many role models out there, so be a role model for others by sharing your experience and knowledge.

Your life has meaning and your actions shape your circumstances. If you live in a free country, you have so much freedom to realize your dreams that one life is hardly enough.

Be grateful and stand up for your ideals. The compass of life lies within you. Use it and you will reach your goal.

Test

You can test yourself every day. Take a situation where things seem to go completely different than you imagined.

A week's vacation, you get up at 4 a.m. and drive to the airport. The bus transfer from the parking lot leaves right in front of you. You still get a taxi and your flight at 5:50am has a two-hour delay, which in the end turns out to be a four-hour one.

Flight time to your holiday resort is only two hours. It is a sunny day and four hours of your deserved holiday have been wasted.

The question is here: How do you deal with this situation?

What can you change about the circumstances?

Only your attitude and your state of mind will allow you to rethink and master the situation. Raising your blood pressure and getting upset does not help. There are much worse things in life.

Then you suddenly see a man in a wheelchair, who is also waiting for the plane. What he would give to be able to walk! What does four hours of waiting mean now?

This is also a test of how you handle time at the airport. The screen with the news is on and you read the latest polls that claim young people are on their mobile phones 58 hours a week. That's almost 8 hours a day! How much of our lifetime is wasted and how much useless content burdens our brain.

Get yourself a coffee and read a book. Write a story about the behavior of the other passengers. Close your eyes and relax also with headphones and music and be grateful when you arrive at your holiday destination healthy after all.

Yes, you have once again experienced live what it is like to have to handle yourself in a situation that was not planned.

Life always has the power to teach us something and we shouldn't take ourselves too seriously as if it were all so unbearable.

Smile at others in this situation and maybe see that a baby close to you does not have all these problems and collects all the impressions because they are new and happy.

Yes, turn your face towards the sun and the shadows will fall behind you. In the movie of your life you are director, producer and leading actor all wrapped into one.

Show what you are capable of and do your best. You have all the skills and should always surprise yourself in a positive fashion.

What have you already experienced and how much have you already achieved?

You will also be able to deal with stressful situations that are not always predictable.

Our perception shapes our truth. How you see, feel and perceive it is your reality.

The man in the wheelchair and the baby have another one. We think everything happens to us, but the things themselves are neutral. Our evaluation and judgment make them what we want to see.

It is a question of interpretation and there is a lot of room for interpretation.

Let's try to think differently and make a game where we slip into a different role and perspective.

We can start a new life tomorrow and leave our old imprints behind. The book *Placebo Effect* by Dr. Joe Dispenza describes in detail how far neuroscience has come today.

The fact is you are the creator of your own life. But far too often we do not use that ability or use the power available to us all.

The so-called applied handbrake prevents us from getting into the flow of life and spreading our wings and flying.

Fears, doubts, worries – the baggage is so heavy that we can hardly move. Drop the worries, reorient yourself, meet new people, make new impressions, get to know new countries. All this helps with starting a new life.

Be brave and have more confidence in yourself. Give that film that is your life excitement and adventure. You are not alone; others before you have done it too.

Your life is a miracle and a secret at the same time. Enjoy your unique way of life and create new situations, which you have always wished and dreamed of in your inner world.

Now we come to the essential part of it all:

Yes, I was in a monastery on your behalf and meditated. But what did I really understand?

I would like to share with you the secrets to life.

The secrets to life

It is really quite simple. You merely have to understand it and follow through:

- do 3 things every day towards your goal
- take a 30-minute walk in the nature
- engage in 15 minutes of mediation
- help someone else
- remain aware and live that awareness
- contribute every day
- spread humor and cheer
- motivate people
- do not to take yourself too seriously
- help and support others
- formulate and live your own dreams

But whatever you do to turn your life toward the better, be consistent and persistent.

Training only once is of no use; reading or writing only once is of no use either. Let your new life be dominated by new habits that will give you a full and rich life.

You can start to put all this new knowledge into practice at any time. It is a deal you make with yourself. Only you get to decide how much you really want it. Make a new start and finally get on the fast track toward improvement in your life.

Yesterday is gone!
Tomorrow is unsure! Now is the only thing we have!

Let us do it. Together we will see that the courage to dare something new will be rewarded in the end. If you are a ship anchored in a harbor, you should think about the fact that ships are not built for this purpose.

Cast off the lines and sail into your adventure called

LIFE!

Then came the

Corona pandemic.

The year 2020 had begun with great hope for many. The transition into a new decade, in which great wishes and expectations lay ahead of us all.

Then it came – the PANDEMIC

as predicted years ago in times of the swine flu and SARS.

A worldwide pandemic that can or will infect and kill millions of people. For the first time mankind remembered the Spanish flu a century ago, when at least 30 million people died.

The memory of the avian flu came back and from one day to the next there was only one topic for the first time worldwide: CORONA. The deadly virus, which reached the world via China, Wuang, could become a deadly threat for every human being.

All other topics worldwide were subordinated to this deadly pandemic. Now it was necessary to prevent the greatest damage to mankind. For the first time in history, all governments agreed on how to deal with this deadly virus, which has spread throughout the planet.

The most experienced scientists, virologists, epidemiologists, etc. were heard and soon plans and guidelines for the containment of the virus were decided. A worldwide lockdown was the logical consequence and a curfew and contact restriction was a consequent step to stop the rapid spread of the deadly virus.

Here one appealed to the reason of the population and all the terrible pictures in the media and the increased death rates in Italy, England and New York made everyone realize that this time it is a deadly pandemic that can affect everyone.

But mainly older people and people with previous conditions. Nursing homes were closed to visitors and the hospitals kept their intensive care units ready for the thousands of cases that might come.

Panic and fear gripped the planet. Young and old, for the first time, everyone was affected. The governments published the current case numbers of the corona crisis on a daily basis through the WHO and the John Hopkins Institute, as well as the Robert Koch Institute in Germany.

We were all instructed daily by scientists what it means for all of us and for each individual. For the first time the world stood together against this invisible deadly enemy called "Corona."

Life came to a standstill. Factories were closed. Schools, kindergartens and public life – everything.

People stayed at home. "Stay at home" became the world's motto and the home office became our new normal. People's fear and panic grew and governments of all countries worked under high pressure to solve the problem.

A vaccine would be on the market in 18 months at the earliest, and warnings of a second or even third wave were issued time and again.

Harvard even declared that this crisis could keep us in check for up to two more years. Bill Gates had already warned of such a global pandemic ten years ago, saying that it could cost millions of people their lives if a vaccine was not found with which seven billion people could and must be vaccinated.

Vaccination was brought into play, as were other restrictions on humanity.

One thing is clear: life on our planet will never be the same.

What this means for the individual and for the whole of humanity could not be guessed in the slightest. Since there were new rules every day and everything was tried to bring order into the unknown, many people were even more uncertain.

Social distancing was the new trend and those who did not keep the minimum distance of 1.5 meters were punished. The police were constantly on duty to control the implementation of the announced measures.

In addition, there was the permanent broadcasting of special TV programs on the subject of "Corona."

As a result, there was the world's first global shutdown, which locked the population in their homes to keep the danger of infection at a minimum. Every day new horrorific numbers and horrible images were broadcast in the media worldwide. We followed the news on an hourly basis on the radio and TV and in addition on social media such as Facebook and YouTube.

Then, of course, soon the other camp arose, which tried to show a differentiated view of the pandemic together with other scientists and virologists.

Comparisons with the avian flu, influenza etc. were made. But the MAINSTREAM was not impressed. The issue was too big to be viewed otherwise.

Finally, from the middle of April onwards, compulsory mask-wearing was introduced, which had previously been described as unhelpful. But now the masks were there. So, now they have to be worn when entering a shop, barbershop etc.

An initial relaxation of the shutdown measures was slowly introduced and you were allowed to meet a contact person outside the family. Bit by bit people went outside again and enjoyed a gradual relaxation of the strict rules during the Corona crisis.

Retail spaces opened up and the cities filled up with people. Take-out gradually emerged and people were waiting for beer gardens and restaurants to open.

The first desire to travel again grew more intense and something like "hope" was born.

A positive aspect to it all? Nature recovered so visibly during the months of the lockdown without air traffic and restricted car traffic that everyone could see it. The weather was extraordinarily wonderful and the silence was indescribable.

Yes, one can and should see every crisis as an opportunity. There was enough time for everyone to evaluate things in a new and different way and to reflect.

How is the new life "post-Corona" supposed to look like? What should really be reconsidered and put to the test? Always faster, further and higher?

Even more consumption?

Or should we stop for a moment and take a thorough inventory of our lives so far and think about what really makes sense in life?

But here too the big question arises:

Are we self-determined or are we other-determined?

Who tells us what we have to do when, how and why?

Is this already the new age with even more technology and monitoring of the individual at any time and any place?

Is humanity now so paralyzed by fear that statements of the second wave in autumn or even the third wave in spring have changed the life of the individual in such a way that fear and panic have become our new life companions?

People who are afraid of other people and within a very short time we have limited or given up our hugs with parents, children and friends because the invisible deadly virus is everywhere.

Much of what we took for granted has become impossible from one day to the next. The feeling of boundless freedom suddenly blown away. No longer simply booking a trip and flying or driving here or there. Absolute reset and restart.

How will a life "post-Corona" or how will a life with "permanent Corona" be?

Which old tracks and habits do we have to let go of?

What will never come back?

But also, what is possible from now on?

Which new opportunities arise for us and for each individual?

How many people will lose their jobs?

How many existences will be destroyed?

Are the economy and politics strong enough to get the coming inferno under control?

What are world politics able to do for humanity with and after Corona?

For each of us it is time for personal stock-taking:

Where do I stand today?
How has my life been so far?
What should my life be like from now on?
What can the individual do?
What can we as a society and community do?

The most important thing first: always think for yourself. We have the ability to think and have the greatest ability to communicate. Now it is up to each individual to think about what all this means. What it does to us, who benefits from it and how strong we are in crises.

Mankind has already been confronted with so many crises, wars, diseases etc. that the question arises even now:

How do we deal with them, what conclusions do we draw from them, what are the consequences for us?

Each individual should think for himself, have an opinion and represent it. In the age of Wikipedia, Google and the Internet, everyone can inform themselves sufficiently and use the time sensibly to form their own opinion about what has happened so apparently "suddenly."

Four things have struck me immensely:

- This time it is something that has happened worldwide and all media are reporting on "Corona."
- Otherwise there were weekly demonstrations for and against everything, from milk prices to climate change – now everyone has fallen silent.
- Even the Catholic Church let Easter, the largest ecclesiastical celebration, passed by without mass and protests. No message that it is the end of the world and Jesus has risen.
- The fact that two years ago almost 25,000 people in Germany died of influenza. Nobody took any measures or tried to inform or even protect the population.

Every day 8,500 children still die of hunger. That's hardly worth a headline. I have some doubts.

No one has dared to raise their voice and the few who have done so on social media have been vilified as conspiracy theorists. You are viewed as disengaged – left, right or insane.

The biggest computer we have is behind our walls. The so-called brain. Turn it on, if it exists, and think for yourself.

The exchange and communication have brought us here in our common way. Let's continue together on the path to a self-determined future.

Where is Generation "Y", the student movements that otherwise always stood up for their future? Everyone has an inner voice and intuition that tells us what we have to change to survive in this new world and to create a better future for all.

The following generations have a right to a self-determined life on planet Earth that we pass on responsibly in the awareness that "There's enough to go around!"

Be the change you want to see in the world
(Mahatma Gandhi).

- Start small, but start making a contribution to humanity and planet Earth
- With all the fear and panic – there is also an invisible God who never lets us down
- Let us use the crisis as an opportunity to change things for the better

So that the
"rest of time"
becomes the
"best of time."

Acknowledgements

A very special thanks to my wife Inge, who provided me so much emotional support throughout the course of this book project to the very end. She motivated me to continue when it became particularly difficult.

I would also like to thank my friend and mentor Josef Schaaf, who showed me the way into the world of books in the first place, as well as Christa Beiling and Claudia Feldten, who always helped me with words and deeds to realize the book.

My special thanks go to my best friend Franz, who passed away last year when he was only 60 years old. He showed us all how important it is to enjoy every moment of life.

Lastly, thanks to all my readers who bought this book and who have benefitted personally from it.

Yours truly,

Ulrich Kellerer